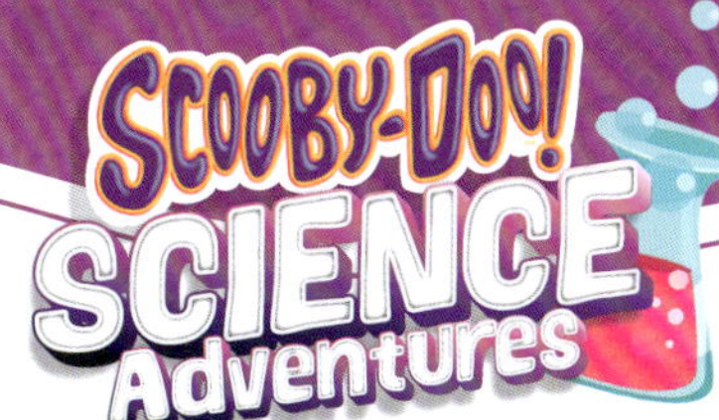

HOLD THE PHONE! The Mystery of Sound!

by Ailynn Collins

CAPSTONE PRESS
a capstone imprint

Published by Capstone Press, an imprint of Capstone
1710 Roe Crest Drive, North Mankato, Minnesota 56003
capstonepub.com

Library of Congress Cataloging-in-Publication Data
is available on the Library of Congress website.

ISBN: 9798875214189 (hardcover)
ISBN: 9798875214264 (paperback)
ISBN: 9798875214271 (ebook PDF)

Summary: Things are moving and grooving as Scooby and the Mystery Inc. gang investigate the secrets of sound. From waves and frequencies to hearing and echoes, uncover the marvelous mysteries of sound.

Editorial Credits
Editor: Christopher Harbo; Designer: Tracy Davies; Media Researcher: Svetlana Zhurkin; Production Specialist: Whitney Schaefer

Image Credits
Getty Images: 500px/Cal Holman, 25, AnatolyM, 11 (diamond), blueringmedia, 22, Maksym Belchenko, 27, massimo colombo, 24, musicinside, 5, Oxford Scientific, 26, ttsz, 18, 21, VectorMine, 16, Winai_Tepsuttinun, 11 (hammer); Shutterstock: Ailisa, 10, AlenKadr, 12 (plastic wrap), Alexander_P, 19, Alexandr Shyripa, 12 (jar), azazello photo studio, 7, Cartooncux (beaker), cover and throughout, Creative Travel Projects, 9, Daisy Daisy, 14, domnitsky, 12 (cereal), Dragon Images, 8, Dream01, 9 (inset), 10 (inset), 11 (top), Feng Yu, 15 (rubber bands), grayjay, 28, HobbitArt (science icons), cover and throughout, Kabardins photo, 15 (tissue box), kearia, 6 (pebbles), Kind fairy, 12 (cell phones), Maria Martyshova (background), cover and throughout, Quang Ho, 12 (rubber bands), Right Perspective Images, 23, Serhii Brovko, cover (sound wave bars), Vaclav Sonnek, 17, Varunyuuu, cover (waves with circles), ViDI Studio, 20, Volcko Mar, 6, Wicaksono_VisualStudio, 26 (sound waves)

Printed and bound in China. PO 006276

Table of Contents

What Is Sound?

On their day off, the Mystery Inc. gang is hanging out at home. Scooby is playing a video game. Shaggy is listening to a podcast on his earbuds. Fred, Daphne, and Velma are dancing to music.

RIIING! RIIING! It's the Mystery Inc. phone.

Hey! Someone needs to get that call! But it's so loud in here, most of the Mystery Inc. gang can't hear the phone ringing. Lucky for them, Scooby has good ears. Without him, they may have missed an important mission!

And that goes to show how important sound is in our world. Every day, we hear all kinds of sounds—loud or soft, pleasant or not so much. But what is sound?

Sound is a form of energy. When you hear the phone ringing or someone singing, energy is transferred to your ears through sound waves.

What does it mean that sound travels in waves? Well, imagine you dropped a pebble into a still pond. What would happen? You'd see ripples form and move away from the spot where the pebble plunked into the water. This is kind of like how sound waves move too.

Hey, Shaggy. If sound travels through air, why don't you wake up when your alarm rings?

Yikes! I must be a *sound* sleeper!

As sound waves travel through the air, we hear them. We can also hear sound waves that travel through solids and liquids.

FACT

Energy is the capacity to do work. There are many types of energy, including electricity, gravity, heat, light, and sound.

Sound Travels in Waves

Hold the phone, gang! What's the science secret behind sound? That's easy! Sound begins when something vibrates or shakes at a very fast speed.

Let's say someone knocks on a door. Their hand hitting the door causes the molecules in the door to vibrate. These vibrations travel through the door's material in waves. The energy from the vibration spreads to neighboring molecules, like tiny rubber balls bouncing off each other.

On the other side of the door, the waves knock into the air molecules, which then vibrate too. These sound waves travel through the air to our ears, so we can hear the knock.

KNOCK! KNOCK!

Roo's there?

Sound flies through the friendly skies!

VROOOOM!

molecules in a gas

The speed at which sound reaches our ears depends on what it is traveling through. When sound waves travel through a gas, such as air, they pass through loosely packed molecules. In room temperature air, sound moves about 1,125 feet (343 meters) per second. If the air is colder, it moves a little slower. If the air is warmer, sound moves a little faster. But these differences are so slight, you wouldn't even notice.

FACT

Because there is no air in outer space, sound has nothing to travel through. No matter how loud you shout in space, no one will hear you!

Do you think sound travels faster through water or air? Did you guess water? Then you are right!

Sound travels faster through liquids than gases because liquid molecules are packed together more closely. The sound waves can pass more quickly from one molecule to the next. The speed of sound through water is 4,859 feet (1,481 m) per second. That's more than four times faster than sound travels through air!

What about when sound travels through solids? You guessed it. Sound moves even faster! That's because the molecules in solids are packed tightly. They help sound waves move super fast.

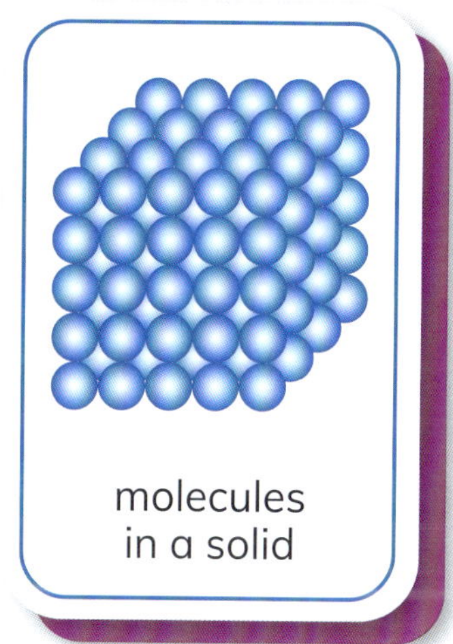
molecules in a solid

How fast, exactly? It depends on the solid. Sound can travel through iron at 16,789 feet (5,117 m) per second. Through a diamond, it travels at an amazing speed of 39,370 feet (12,000 m) per second. Wow!

Whoa! That's some supersonic bling, Scoob!

TING! TING!

FACT

Did you know that elephants can feel sound vibrations with their feet? They can "hear" them from up to 20 miles (32 kilometers) away!

Visible Vibrations

WHAT YOU'LL NEED

2 cell phones

large jar

plastic wrap

string or rubber bands

small cereal pieces

WHAT TO DO

1. Place one cell phone inside the jar with its ringer set to play out loud.
2. Cover the mouth of the jar tightly with plastic wrap. Use string or rubber bands to hold it in place.
3. Place some small cereal pieces on top of the plastic wrap.
4. Use the second cell phone to call the cell phone inside the jar. Let it ring.

What happened? Did the cereal pieces dance around? If so, you saw sound waves in action! They caused the plastic wrap to vibrate and the cereal to dance.

Loud and Soft Sounds

Alright, gang! We know sound travels in waves, but have you ever wondered why sounds are soft or loud? Well, the science behind this mystery is called volume. Volume is the loudness or softness of a sound. And volume depends on the size—or amplitude—of a sound wave's vibration.

What would amplitude look like if you could see it? Just imagine waves at the beach. Some are tall, some are short. Their height is the amplitude. The greater the amplitude, the louder the sound.

Look, Scoob! It's like I'm surfing a louder sound!

Hee-hee-hee-hee-hee!

Hey, gang! We know sounds can be loud or soft. But what makes them high or low? This mystery involves pitch.

Pitch is how fast or slow vibrations are moving. When there are more, or faster, vibrations happening in one second, a sound's pitch is higher. A low-pitched sound has slower vibrations.

Pitch-Perfect Guitar

WHAT YOU'LL NEED

empty tissue box

rubber bands of different thicknesses

WHAT TO DO

1. Remove all the plastic from the opening in the tissue box.
2. Wrap rubber bands of different thickness around the tissue box. Make sure each one crosses over the opening in the box and space them apart so they don't touch.
3. Pluck each rubber band one at a time. Which ones have higher pitches? Which ones have lower pitches?
4. Rearrange the rubber bands so they go from lowest to highest pitch.

Just like on a guitar, the thicker bands have a lower pitch than the thinner ones. This is because the thicker bands vibrate at a slower speed.

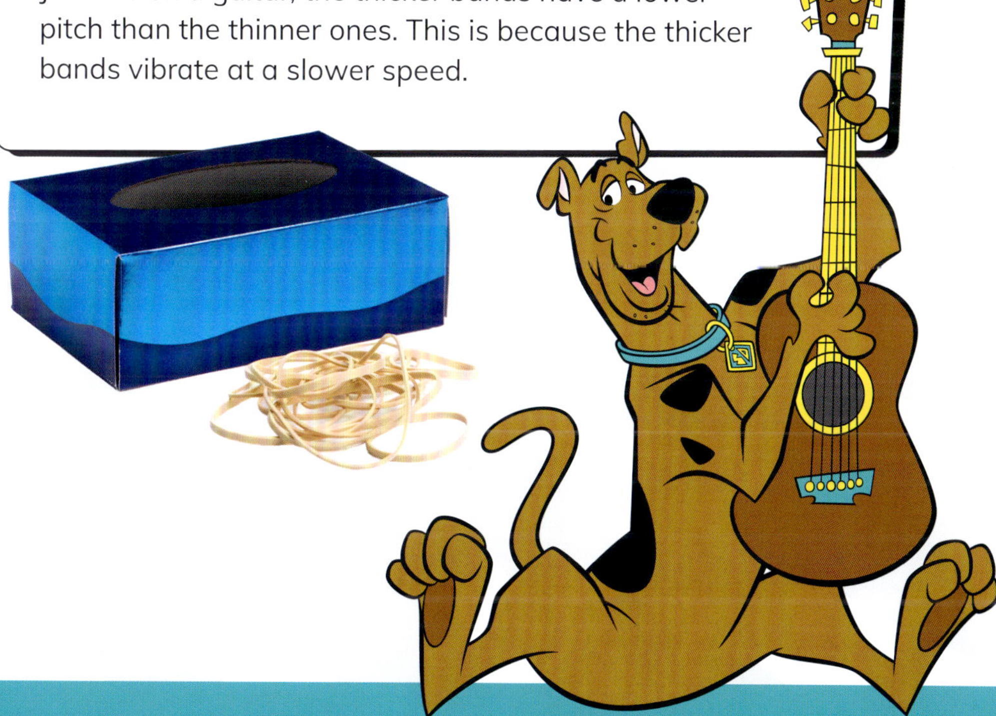

Remember how the pitch of a sound is about the speed of the vibrations? Well, that speed has a special name—it's called the frequency. The number of waves a sound makes per second is its frequency.

In science, we say that high-pitched sounds that vibrate many times per second have a high frequency. When a low sound vibrates more slowly, we say it has a low frequency.

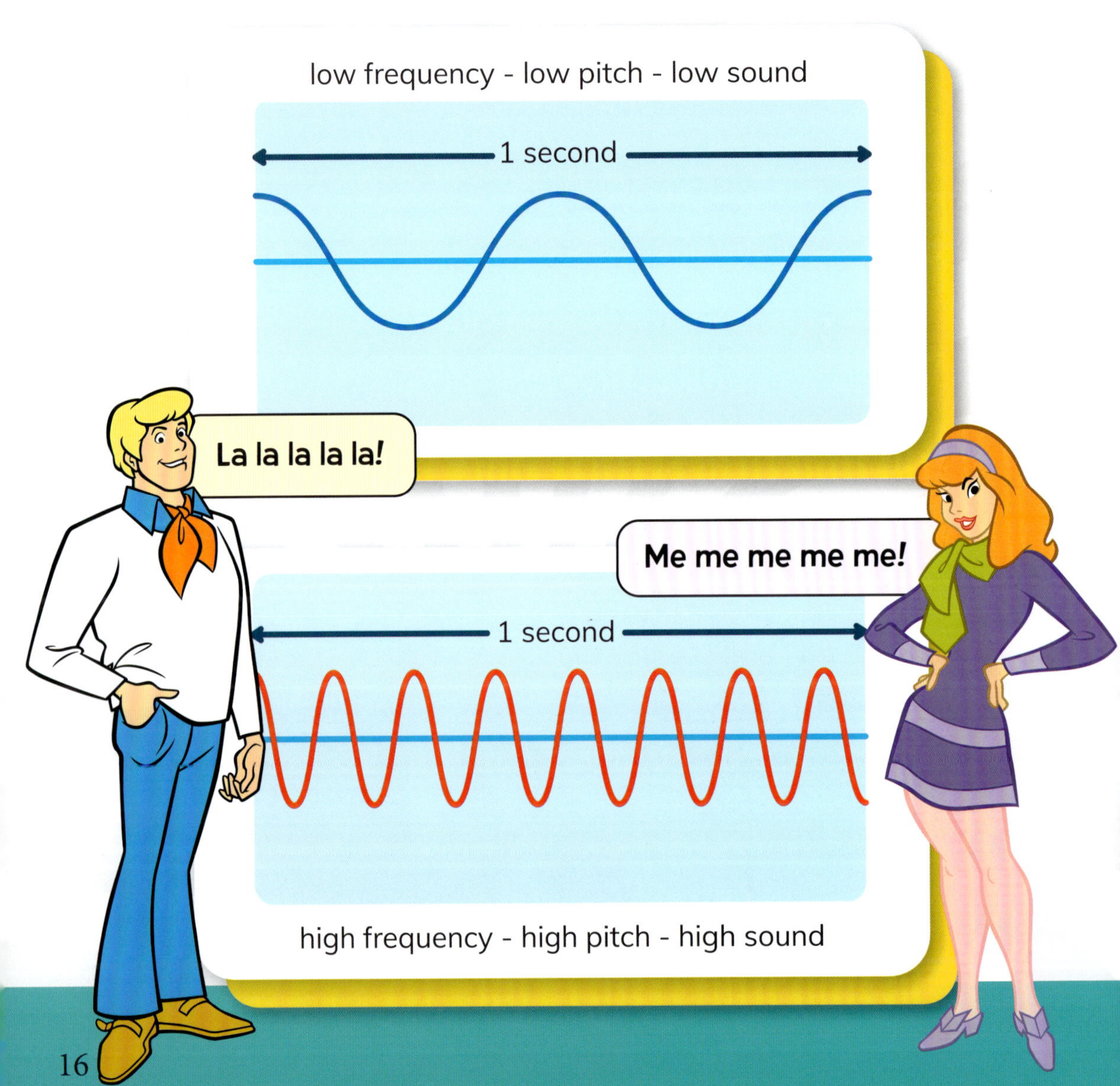

We measure frequency using units called hertz (Hz). A sound vibration that happens once every second has a frequency of 1 Hz. A frequency of 100 Hz means that the sound vibrates 100 times per second.

Humans can hear frequencies up to 20,000 Hz. But animals can hear sounds at even higher frequencies. Dogs, like Scooby, can hear frequencies as high as 47,000 to 65,000 Hz! Some sounds, like dog whistles, have such a high frequency that only dogs can hear them.

Sounds and the Human Body

Listen up, gang! We've learned a lot about sound so far. Now, let's talk about the sounds we make with our voices and how we hear them.

When it comes to our voices, our respiratory system plays a big part in the sounds we make. Whether whispering, talking, laughing, or crying, it all starts with breathing. When we breathe in, air rushes into our mouths, passes through the larynx, and travels into our lungs.

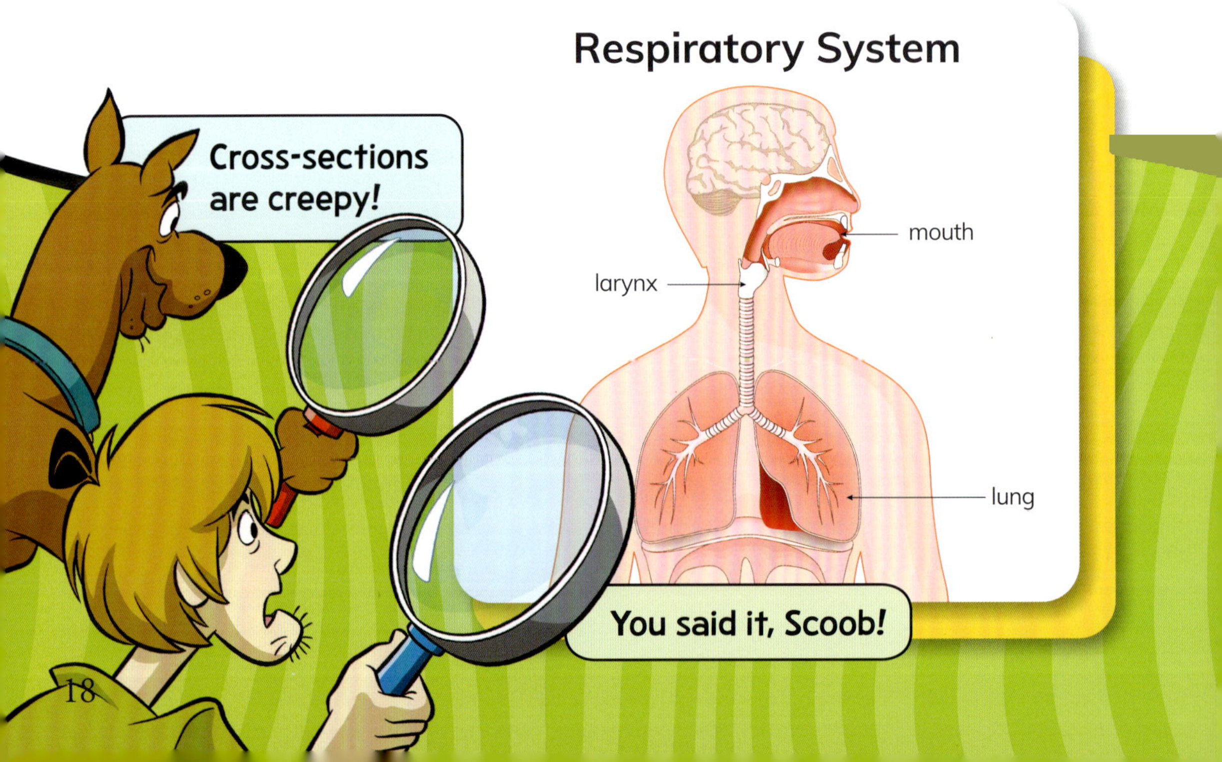

Cross-sections are creepy!

Respiratory System

mouth

larynx

lung

You said it, Scoob!

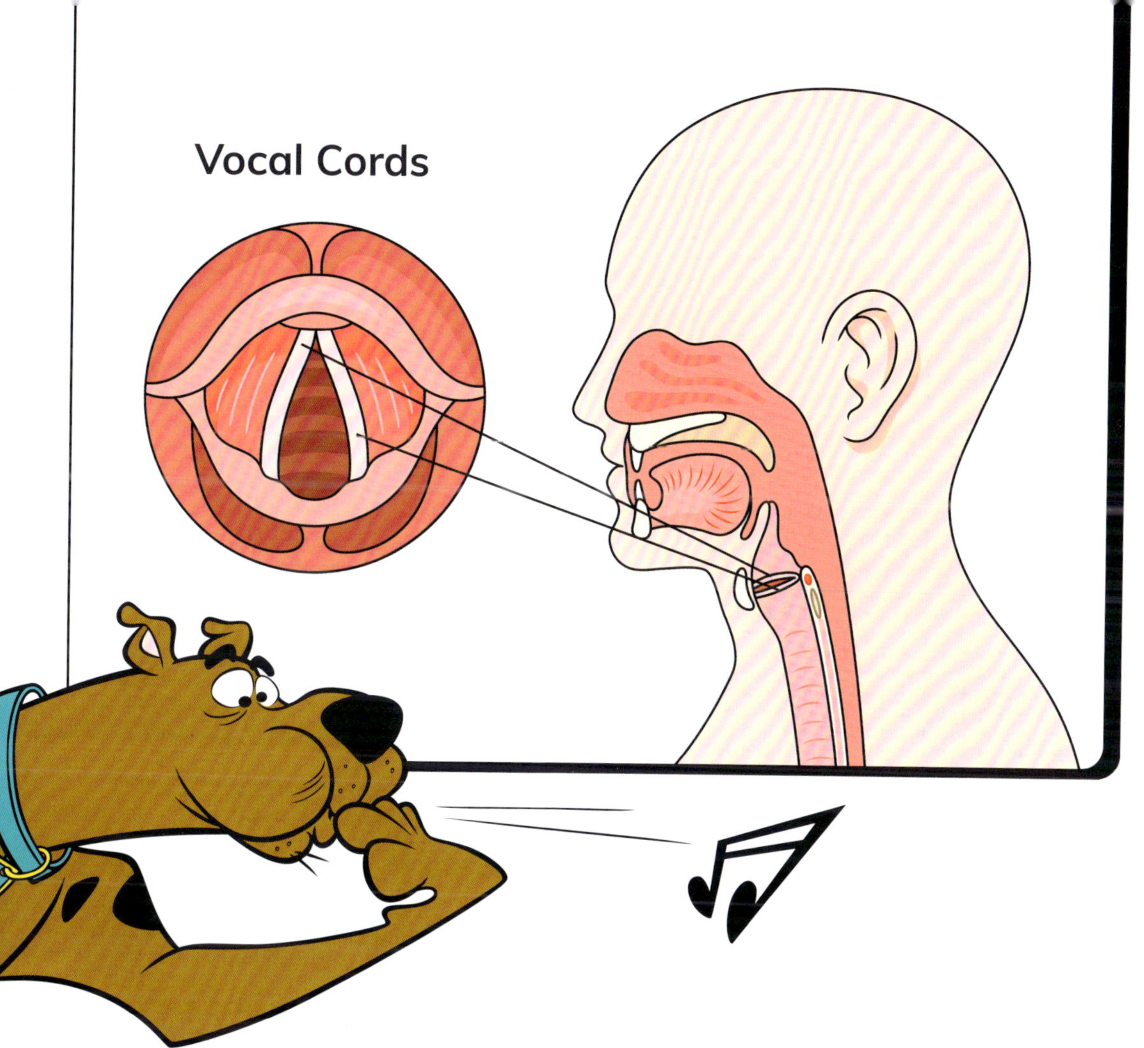

When you breathe out, air passes back through the larynx—and this is where the magic happens. The larynx, which is also called the voice box, contains vocal cords. As air passes over these cords, they vibrate. These vibrations create sound waves! Then your tongue and lips move to make certain sounds with these waves. These sounds are words that others can understand.

Now that we know how we make sounds, let's talk about how we hear them. What are those flappy things on the sides of your head? Here's a clue. Scooby's are bigger than the rest of the Mystery Inc. gang's.

You're right! They're ears! Our ears have many parts that help us hear. When a sound happens, its waves enter the outer ear. Then they travel through the ear canal until they hit the eardrum.

The eardrum vibrates when sound waves hit it. These vibrations then travel to the middle ear where three tiny bones make them louder. Then the vibrations move into the inner ear where a spiral-shaped cochlea turns them into electrical signals. These signals head to a nerve that carries them to the brain. Faster than we can even think about it, the brain helps us understand the sound.

Anatomy of the Ear

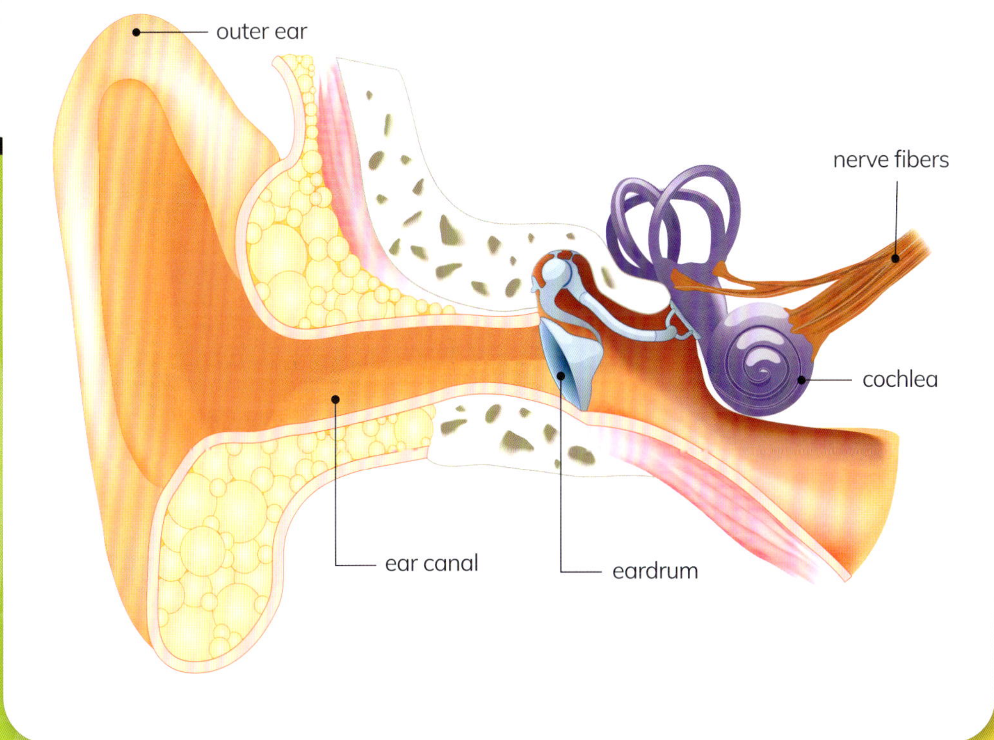

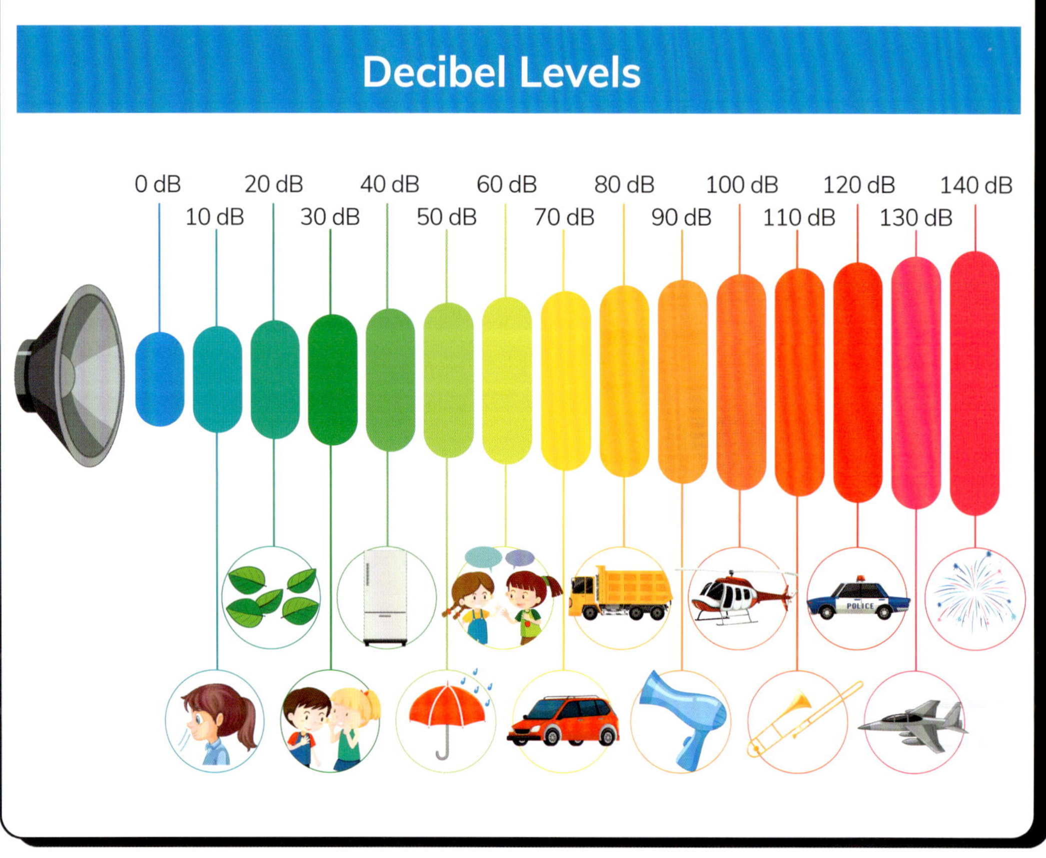

Wow! That was quite a journey for those little sound waves. But did you know that the intensity of a sound can have a big impact on your ears? A unit called the decibel (dB) is used to measure how intense a sound is. It tells us how much energy a sound wave has.

At a normal volume, talking measures at about 60 dB. A quiet whisper is about 30 dB. Fireworks measure at around a whopping 140 dB.

Sounds that measure more than 85 dB can really hurt our ears. Listening to loud sounds for a long time can even cause us to lose our hearing. The louder the sounds, the less time it takes to damage the ears permanently.

So, protect your ears! Use ear plugs or protective headphones when you are around loud sounds for a long time. And don't listen to loud music for too long. Take a moment to enjoy the quiet.

Echo! Echo! Echo!

The Mystery Inc. gang is out on a hike today. At the top of a hill, they stop to admire the view. Shaggy shouts "hello" into the distance. "Hello, hello, hello," he hears a voice call back to him. What just happened?

The sound of Shaggy's voice bouncing back is called an echo. Echoes happen when sounds bounce off smooth, hard surfaces, like walls, or the sides of a mountain.

Echoes aren't just fun and games. They are also super useful—especially to animals that use them!

That's right! Bats use echoes to fly and hunt at night. Dolphins use them to swim through the ocean. And shrews need echoes to find their food. But how do they do it?

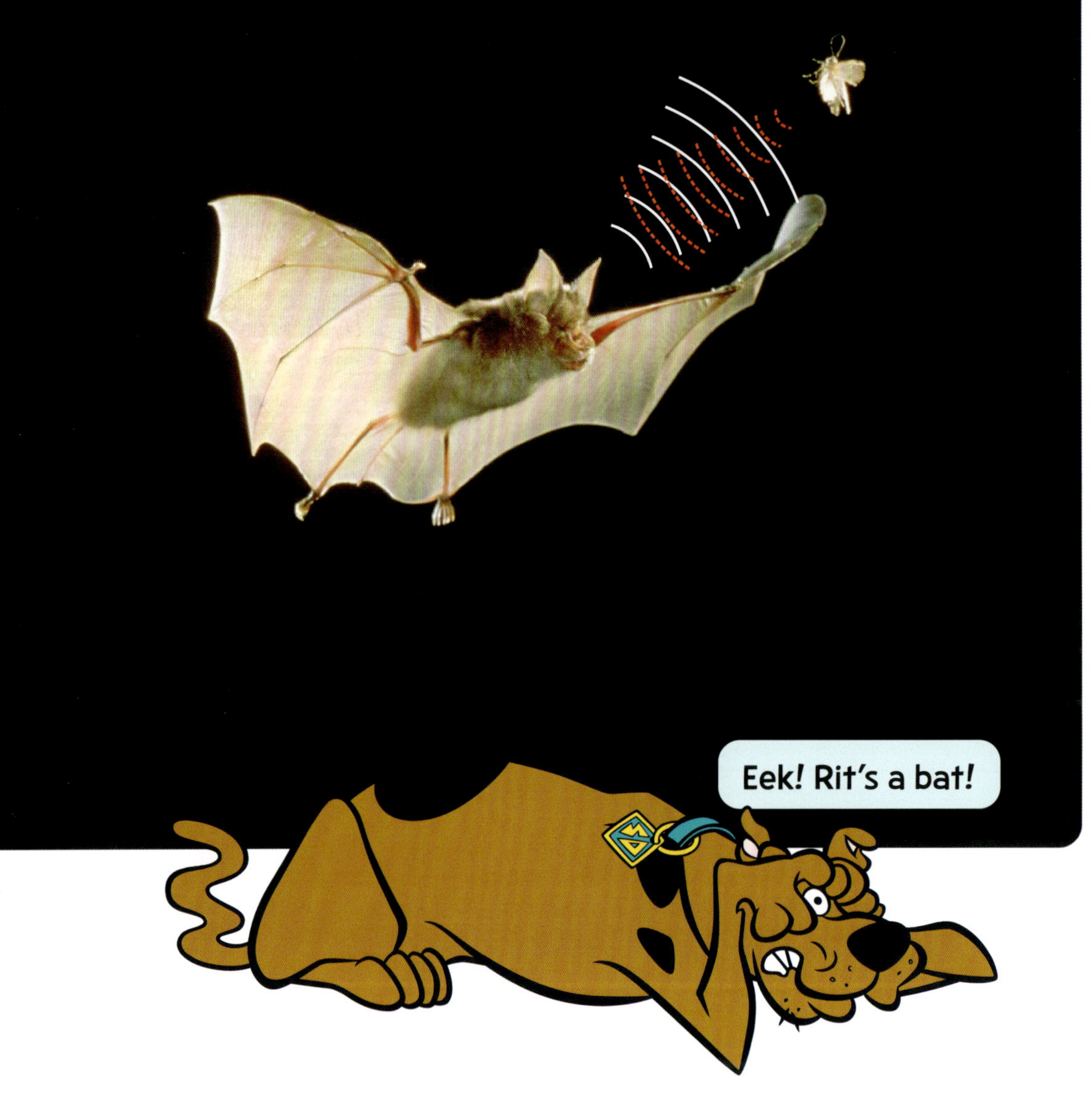

Creatures that use echoes have a skill called echolocation. With it, they send out high-pitched sounds that bounce against anything hard. These can be big things like trees and rocks or small ones like birds and bugs. When the sound bounces back to them, the animal can tell where the objects are located.

Animals aren't the only ones who get in on the echo action. Doctors do too! They use echoes to see inside our bodies with ultrasound machines. These machines send high-frequency sounds into the body. When the waves bounce back, they give doctors a picture of what's inside.

People also use echoes to "see" underwater. Many large ships use sonar—Sound Navigation and Ranging—equipment. This equipment works much like echolocation. It sends sound waves through the water to bounce off objects. When the sound waves return, they reveal the distance and size of the objects. Sonar can even show the shape of an object.

Many fishing ships use sonar to find fish. The military uses sonar to detect enemy submarines.

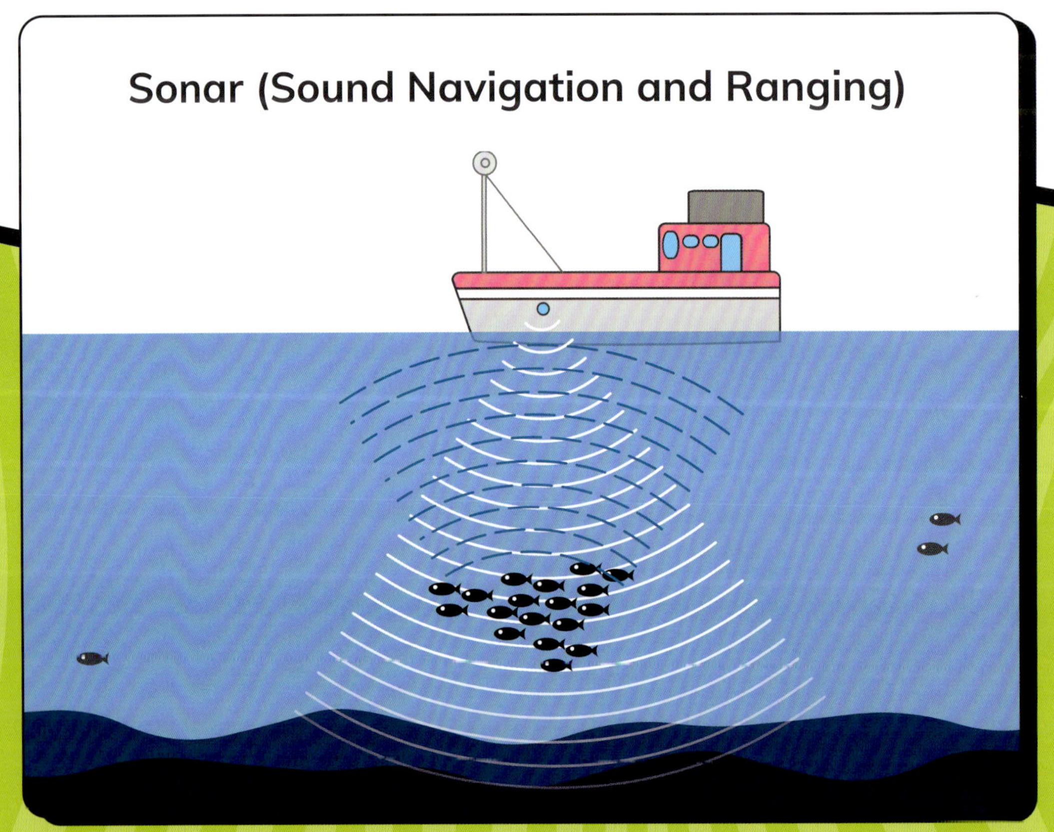

From molecules and frequencies to voice boxes and echoes, the science of sound is all around us. The next time you call out to your friends, hear a bird chirp, or enjoy a concert, think about how those sound waves and vibrations travel through your ears to your brain. Marvel at how some animals can hear so much more.

And don't forget to keep those ears safe by turning down loud sounds. They are the only ears you've got!

GLOSSARY

amplitude (AM-pluh-tude)—a measure of wave strength

decibel (DE-suh-buhl)—a unit for measuring the volume of sounds

echolocation (eh-koh-loh-KAY-shuhn)—the process of using sounds and echoes to locate objects

frequency (FREE-kwuhn-see)—the number of sound waves that pass a location in a certain amount of time

hertz (HURTS)—a unit for measuring the frequency of sound wave vibrations; one hertz equals one sound wave per second

molecule (MOL-uh-kyool)—a group of two or more atoms making up the smallest unit of a substance

nerve (NURV)—a thin fiber that sends messages between the brain and other parts of the body

pitch (PICH)—how high or low a sound is

sonar (SOH-nar)—a device that uses sound waves to find underwater objects

ultrasound (UHL-truh-sound)—sound that is too high for humans to hear that can be used for medical scans

vibration (vye-BRAY-shuhn)—a fast movement back and forth

READ MORE

Lundgren, Julie K. *Sound: Hear All About It*. New York: Crabtree Publishing, 2022.

Midthun, Joseph. *Sound*. Chicago: World Book, 2022.

Turner, Myra Faye. *Investigating Sound in Max Axiom's Lab*. North Mankato, MN: Capstone Press, 2025.

INTERNET SITES

Britannica Kids: Sound
kids.britannica.com/kids/article/sound/353791

Ducksters: Physics for Kids—Basics of Sound
ducksters.com/science/sound101.php

Time for Kids: Science of Sound
timeforkids.com/k1/science-sound

INDEX

ABOUT THE AUTHOR

Ailynn Collins has written many books for children, from stories about aliens and monsters, to books about science, space, and the future. These are her favorite subjects. She lives outside Seattle with her family and five dogs. When she's not writing, she enjoys participating in dog shows and dog sports.